Gus Looks for Dad

By Sally Cowan

Gus had torn his wing on a net in the storm.

His wing still felt stiff and sore.

And it was a bit short!

Gus missed his dad!

He flew off the rocks
to look for him.

But Gus would not need
to fly a long way.

Gus got a big shock
at the port!

The shed had been torn down.
Dad was not there!

Gus went to the chip store.

A big gull pecked at
a corn cob.

"Have you seen my dad?"
Gus said.

"No!" the gull yelled.
"And get away from my corn!"

Gus flew up and down
the shore looking for Dad.

He was sad and wanted
to cry!

Oh! I will look for Dad at the cliffs!
We were there when the storm hit.

Gus went up high.

His short wing was not too sore, so he did a big glide.

But he did not see Dad.

Gus got very hungry!

He went down to the shore
to grab a crab.

Then ...

"Gus! Gus!" yelled Dad.

Gus and Dad had a big hug.

"See this shack by the shore?"
said Dad.
"It's home!"

And for the rest of the day,
Gus and Dad had more
crabs and more clams!

CHECKING FOR MEANING

1. How did Gus tear his wing? *(Literal)*

2. Where did Gus find Dad? *(Literal)*

3. How do you think Gus felt when he talked to the gull with the corn? *(Inferential)*

EXTENDING VOCABULARY

port	What is a *port*? What might you see at a port?
shore	What does the word *shore* mean? How is this different from the word *sure*? Use both in a sentence.
cliffs	Where would you find *cliffs*? What words could you use to describe a cliff?

MOVING BEYOND THE TEXT

1. What do seagulls look like? What do they sound like?

2. How would you describe how seagulls behave?

3. What should you do if you get separated from the adults you are with?

4. What can we do to keep beach wildlife safe?

SPEED SOUNDS

ar	er	ir	ur	or

storm

torn

short

port

for

corn

sore

store

shore

more